BLOOM &
grow

Life Lessons from
a Montana Garden

REFLECTIONS & PHOTOGRAPHY BY KAREEN BRATT

Published by Mrs. Kareen Ann Bratt
Somers, Montana
ISBN: 978-1467992008
Printed in USA

Acknowledgements:
Words and photography by Kareen Bratt
Edited and encouraged by Jo Alice Juedeman
Graphic Design by Joellyn Clark

Bible references from New International Version
and King James Version

to Glee

"Life has taught us that love does not consist of gazing at each other but in looking outward in the same direction."

~Anais Nin

Contents

Believe

In the fall I cut back and divided my geraniums, moving them indoors to a south window. But I didn't have the heart to cut back these two stunning geraniums. Would it be possible, I wondered, to keep them blooming and growing through the winter months?

Indirect lighting and lots of water did the trick. Side by side, the two geraniums grew to about three feet tall, with compact vibrant green leaves and masses of soft pink and rich rose colored flowers.

The first warm spring day I moved the heavy pot with its cheerful blossoms outside, onto our covered front porch. But it was too early. I awoke a few mornings later to an unexpected heavy frost and my beautiful geraniums frozen to the core of their being. I now had no choice but to cut back the plants, bring them into the house and return them to the sunny south window of my dining room. But would they recover? I had my doubts.

Surprisingly, green leaves were soon sprouting from the remaining stems. It took all summer, but sunshine, water and the inner strength of the plants themselves, gradually brought about the glorious rebirth of both damaged geraniums.

Life is like that. Sometimes we feel like it's all over. Events have damaged our hearts, freezing the life out of us. But by carefully and selectively pruning away the hurt, anger and disappointment, all the while believing in the good that God has placed around us and yes, even within us, we will thrive and bloom once again. Believe in yourself. Believe in others. Believe in Him.

"Jesus said to her, "I am the resurrection and the life. He who believes in me will live, even though he dies..."

believe ~ geranium

"And be kind to one another, tenderhearted, forgiving one another, even as God for Christ's sake has forgiven you."

Ephesians 4:32

tenderhearted ~ bleeding heart

Tenderhearted

Bleeding Hearts are among the most graceful yet resilient flowers in the garden. The slightest breeze causes the fragile heart shaped blooms to ripple gently from the tiny tendrils that connect each of them to the main stem. Yet, even a severe wind fails to break that same tenuous connection.

I was first attracted to this plant as a young girl wandering in my Grandmother's garden. Its beauty and dramatic name stoked my adolescent imagination. Visions of broken and bleeding hearts spoke to me of romance, heartache and unrequited love. Today I understand that a bleeding, damaged heart eventually dies. But a tender heart survives and even thrives.

Weathering the crosswinds of life by implementing our God given gifts of grace, flexibility and endurance, we can overcome our own heartaches and help heal the hurt of others.

A tender heart, recalling its own pain and disappointment, is able to comfort and console the bleeding heart of another. A tender heart listens with understanding and compassion. Kindness and forgiveness helps ease the ache of a broken heart. God grant us all tender hearts.

*"For I determined not to know anything while with you
except Jesus Christ & Him crucified."*

Determined

After Mother died several years ago, I dug up some perennials from her eastern Montana garden and moved them to my home on the western slope of the Rockies. One of those transplants was a spindly little clematis vine I didn't have much hope for. But come spring, there it was, forcing its way up through the soil, searching desperately for something to grab on to.

Instinctively, I planted a stick in the ground beside the curly vine. Within a day or so it had taken hold and was beginning its climb all the way up to the surrounding lattice, where it anchored itself and has been producing a bounty of blooms ever since.

Oftentimes we feel like we are dying on the vine, unable to accomplish anything of importance or substance. Life seems to have lost its zing and purpose. We fall down; struggle back to our feet only to wander aimlessly, to and fro, without a goal in sight.

That's when it's time to reach out. Grab on to something worthwhile and hold on. A small task, close to home, is a good place to start. Is there a closet that needs cleaning, a flower bed that should be weeded or an elderly neighbor who needs a meal? Determine to do what you can. Keep climbing. Help will come!

Acknowledge

I read about the upcoming 10th anniversary celebration in our local newspaper. As the former director of the program, I waited for an invitation that did not come.

"No big deal," I told myself. "The new faces at the agency probably don't even remember me, let alone that I sweated blood and tears just to get the project off the ground."

A few weeks later, Peter, the out-of-state consultant who had worked with me putting the program together, called. He and the current director, embarrassed at overlooking my invitation, wanted to stop out for a visit.

After exchanging memories of our struggles and victories, Peter said goodbye with a parting gift of six hybrid tulip bulbs he had developed himself.

Each spring when those beautiful, long stemmed, graceful tulips bloom, I am reminded of the anxiety, stress, and sleepless nights I endured in order to accomplish something important. Peter had given me a living reminder of one of my best efforts.

Acknowledging another's achievements and accomplishments need not be a big deal. It doesn't take much to make someone feel worthwhile and appreciated. A kind word, a small gift, or a simple thank you will do. We will see the world differently when we consistently acknowledge the good work of others.

"*In all your ways acknowledge Him, and He will make your paths straight.*"

PROVERBS 3:6

acknowledge ~ hybrid tulip   13

"...be content with what you have, because God has said,
'Never will I leave you; never will I forsake you.'"

Hebrews 13:5

content ~ columbine

Content

Some flowers are very demanding and cranky. In order to get the best from these high-maintenance plants the gardener, the soil, the light and even the air must cater to their every whim. Not so with the lowly columbine. In spite of difficult circumstances, it grows and thrives without attention or pampering.

For years I struggled with the flower bed that extends across the west end of our deck. Nearly every plant tried there has refused to co-exist with the huge pine tree rising up from the center of the bed. First, there are the spreading pine boughs that prevent rain from falling through to the soil. Secondly, toxic pine needles affect the more finicky plants like poison. Lastly, there is the heat of the afternoon sun to contend with.

The columbine takes on all these hazards and keeps on blooming. Contented and satisfied with slim resources, the columbine flourishes under and around the pine tree, producing pink, purple and white flowers for several months each spring.

Can we, like the columbine, do our best under difficult conditions? Do we rise to life's challenges with serenity and poise or are we prone to whine and complain when we encounter bumps and potholes along life's pathway?

Because we live in an imperfect world, it is necessary to learn how to be quietly happy and satisfied. Conditions will not always be ideal; yet we must find a way to grow and thrive in spite of difficult circumstances. A spirit of contentment allows us to embrace tranquility and set our priorities in order.

Shine

Garden magazines, while expensive, help stimulate the gardener's creativity. That's how I first learned about "moonlight gardens". The idea is to plant a border of white flowers along walkways so that, in the darkness, the light of the moon will reflect off the white blooms, illuminating the path.

The fun has been finding white perennials and tucking them into the border: rock cress, bugbane, candytuft, speedwell, peonies, delphinium, obedient plant and phlox to name a few. An iceberg rose blooms most of the summer. Annuals, such as cosmos, snapdragons, petunias and alyssum fill in the gaps.

Regardless of the moon's phase, the white blooms gather up moonbeams and shine them softly back into the dark night, lighting the way for all who travel the path to and from my front door.

We should do likewise. In a world that has its share of darkness, doubt and despair we can reflect encouragement, kindness and goodness. We can light the way for those who are discouraged and fearful. Our thoughtfulness can, in a small way, replicate God's love, causing it to shine even when life's pathway seems the darkest.

"…let your light shine before men, that they may see your good deeds and praise your Father in heaven."

Faithful

My showy peony has been faithfully blooming every spring since we moved here over thirty years ago and, because our home is an old farm property, for many years before that. Through good conditions and bad, it has done its best to exceed our expectations. A little compost, a little water, lots of sunshine and, without fail, the lovely pink flowers with the bright yellow centers continues to charm us each and every June.

Faithfulness is a quiet quality not often appreciated until we are confronted with unfaithfulness. The discovery of betrayal is an earthshaking event, fraught with recriminations, withdrawal and regrets. Only in the absence of faithfulness do we realize the benefit of steadfast friends, confidants and family members. Trust in those closest to us fosters a sense of well-being, peace of mind and confidence. Faithfulness acts as a buffer against the duplicity and treachery of the outside world.

Being faithful is not easy. It means always coming through; always being there, every time, without fail. "Always" is hard. Faithfulness is not optional if we are to build intimacy and trust. Expecting loyalty from others we can only demand it of ourselves.

How sweet is a relationship when faithfulness is unwavering!

"Now it is required that those who have been given a trust must prove faithful."

I CORINTHIANS 4:2

faithful ~ peony

"A man's wisdom gives him patience; it is to his glory to overlook an offense."

patience ~ impatiens

PROVERBS 19:11

Patience

Take a good look. These are the only impatiens I've ever been able to grow that lasted beyond June. At this point in time, I have lost patience with impatiens. My daughter has the secret, growing banks of these lovely flowers in her entryway planter. So far, I have not been able to successfully apply her techniques to the impatiens in my yard.

I have pointed their happy little faces to the east and to the west. I have kept their bed wet and allowed it to dry out. I have planted them late. I have planted them early. My pretty little impatiens struggle, turn brown, spindly and then die. Should I keep trying or plant something else?

Patience is a virtue we all aspire to but seldom master. Underestimating the task at hand is usually our first mistake. Time, sweat, devotion and the "right tool" is required to accomplish anything of value, be it fixing the toaster or mending a relationship.

Sooner or later, patience wears thin and we consider calling for help or abandoning the task altogether. Confidence in our problem solving abilities is shaken. Maybe we should be investing our time and talent in something more productive. That's when we need to take a break.

So next spring I will ignore those lovely masses of pink, white and rose colored flowers at my local garden center. I will roll my cart right on by ... and then, most likely, I'll make a u-turn and come back through. Maybe this year will be different!

"… if you have faith as small as a mustard seed, you can say to this mountain, 'Move from here to there' and it will move. Nothing will be impossible for you."

MATTHEW 17:20

Move on (if you must)

I was emphatic. Only English roses would do for the flower bed adjacent to our front porch. With a southern exposure I was certain it would be the perfect place for the perfect flower. The sight and scent of those lovely roses would be one of the first things to greet our many visitors.

I bought six roses. Because of my inexperience and cautions from other rose growers, I followed the planting directions exactly as specified on the containers. By fall, all six were dying or dead in spite of the many and varied remedies I tried all summer long. I planted six more the following spring and was in the process of losing them when I read, in one of my garden books, that roses do not like to be watered from overhead. A light went on in my brain. Rain, dripping from the porch roof overhang, was falling directly on and around my roses. Straightaway, I grabbed a shovel and moved the three remaining roses to a bed away from the porch.

They responded like magic, doing what roses do best, tantalizing the eye as well as the nose. "Move me, move me," they had been screaming, but I had not been paying attention.

Many of life's difficult situations can be neutralized by moving on. While standing our ground is admirable in most situations, it can prove deadly in other circumstances. The steady drip, drip, drip of conflict, bitterness and resentment quenches the spirit and will eventually destroy the abundant life God has planned for each of us. Pray for the wisdom to know when to give in or, if you must, when to give up and move on.

Hospitality

This painted daisy irritated me every time I laid eyes on it. It wasn't the daisy's fault. I was the one who had planted it next to a rust colored boulder in the back yard. The hot pink of the flower and the orange hue of the rock appeared to be quarreling and I knew I was responsible for the discord. I should have moved the plant, but it was just one of those tasks I didn't get around to, which only added to my irritation.

And so, I ignored the daisy's attempts to charm me, promising myself that I would move it next spring. In the meantime, orange and pink would just have to fight it out.

But one day, as I prowled the yard with my camera, I spotted a butterfly making itself at home on the daisy. Reacting quickly, I snapped the shot and went on my way. Later, when I downloaded the picture to my computer, the orange butterfly and the pink daisy created a vision of harmony and beauty, rather than discord and conflict. The scene was enhanced by bold purples and greens in the background, blocking the rusty boulder from view.

Hospitality is like the daisy and the butterfly. Our surroundings change when we open our door to others. The house is cleaner, the meals tastier, and our conversations elevated. For a while our efforts are focused on others. To our guests, our imperfections are minimized and our hospitality appreciated.

Now is the time to invite others into our life. A simple dish, a comfortable chair; a warm embrace blesses the guest as well as the host. Of course it will take some time, some extra work and expense but "great is our reward" when we make others feel at home.

"Share with God's people who are in need. Practice hospitality."

ROMANS 12:13

hospitality ~ painted daisy

"...Her aim is to be devoted to the Lord
in both body and spirit."

I CORINTHIANS 7:34

Devoted

A birthday celebration is a mother's annual endeavor to prove her undying devotion to each of her children. Without fanfare or appreciation, her offspring accept the meals, clean clothes, transportation and warm beds their mother provides each and every day of the year. The arrival of a birthday, however, raises their expectations of the family matriarch.

My Mother made sure I always had a birthday cake. It wasn't easy since my big day usually fell during harvest, a busy time for a wheat rancher's wife. And the day was always hot, too hot to turn on the oven. On most of my birthdays the closest thing I had to a party was a kitchen full of tired hired men in from the fields for the noon meal. The high point of the party was when my family and the harvest crew sang "Happy Birthday" as I blew out the candles on the angel food cake

Mom had managed to make early that morning.

A small vase, containing freshly picked sweet peas, was placed in the center of the cake, an oasis of color in its cloud-like whipped cream topping. As I look back, I wonder if the flowers weren't a timesaving measure. Feeding a crew of hired men three hot meals a day allowed little time for cake decorating. But my mother's tender cake and the fragrant sweet peas, along with a candle for each year, was confirmation enough of her love and devotion.

What besides the family unit is worthy of our devotion? Today, many causes clamor for our commitment: the schools, the environment, sports and world hunger to name only a few. Let's keep it simple. Devotion to the "good and perfect will of God" ought to cover it, don't you think?

Submit

Zinnias are not soft, delicate flowers. They are tough, stiff and unbending. In spite of those drawbacks, I love this sturdy, hot weather flower. A few scattered seeds in the spring produce, by August, a massive array of luminous blooms growing skyward, reaching for the sun.

As summer comes to a close and I busy myself harvesting the last of my vegetable garden, the surrounding zinnias flaunt their true colors. Their vibrant, dazzling beauty, intensified by the crisp, cool days of autumn, signals the end of the growing season. With one last "hurrah", these robust, dependable flowers seem to be preparing themselves for the soon-to-arrive killer frost.

Protecting the zinnias becomes my mission in life. Blankets and tarps are spread over them every evening as I attempt to extend their growing season just one more day. Eventually though, I must submit to the dictates of "Mother Nature". Frost and freezing temperatures succeed in turning my zinnias into a brown, crumbly mass. There is nothing left to do but pull them out of the ground, harvest some seed and throw the residue on my fall bonfire.

At one time or another, each of us, some more frequently than others, must submit to forces greater than our own. It is not easy to "fight city hall", to push back the inevitable. Whether it's illness, a demanding relative, a recession or a lost argument, our options are usually limited to changing our own attitude and perspective.

Submission is not the same as giving in or giving up. Submission is a choice. When we choose to submit because it makes sense, because it's the right thing to do, or because others will benefit, we maintain our dignity and self-respect. If it helps, think of it as "cooperating".

Much of life is dictated by events beyond our control. The key is to relax; to go with the flow. An old 50's song is a good reminder: "What will be, will be, Que sera, sera".

"Submit to one another out of reverence for Christ."

Ephesians 5:21

Give

Can you imagine a farmstead in summer without a bank of tall, bright sunflowers? Neither could I. In my mind's eye, I pictured yellow, brown, and copper sunflowers clustered around our farm's outbuildings. However, various attempts at strategically planting seeds between the big red barn and our driveway yielded very poor results. Perhaps it was too dry out there beyond the sprinkler system or maybe the seeds were choked out by fast growing weeds. Whatever the cause, I eventually gave up on sunflowers.

Then one warm spring morning, while hoeing my vegetable garden, I spotted something green, stout, and unrecognizable, growing in the middle of my onion sets. I decided to take a detour around the little plants, let them grow and see what developed.

As the season progressed, I finally realized they were sunflowers. Like an unexpected gift, I was blessed, by the end of July, with a beautiful stand of volunteer sunflowers, about five feet tall, right there in the middle of my onions.

Today I don't buy sunflower seeds. I simply watch for the volunteer seedlings and let them do their thing (as long as they do it out by the barn). Be it the wind or birds, volunteer seeds find friendly soil, germinate, take root and, without effort or expense on my part, give me something I could not accomplish on my own: glorious, late blooming sunflowers.

Our world has many needs. We are a blessed people, planted in the middle of a hurting, desperate global community. We all have something to offer. Giving of our time, money and expertise will yield a harvest of joy and good will, impacting our neighbors both near and far. *"Give and it will be given to you, a good measure, pressed down, shaken together and running over." Luke 6:38*

"Freely you have received, freely give."

MATTHEW 10:8

give ~ sunflower   *31*

*"Restore to me
the joy of your
salvation and
grant me a
willing spirit to
sustain me."*

Psalm 51:12

willing ~ dahlia

Willing

I've become possessive over the years. Due to my hard work and vision, the yard, as I saw it, was my domain. My husband, whose passion was fishing, showed little interest in what happened in the garden and flower beds unless, of course, I recruited him for some back-breaking, labor-intensive assistance. So, why his sudden interest in dahlias? The answer was his new fishing buddy, an expert on dahlias, who didn't have enough room to grow them himself.

Their proposal consisted of plowing up another acre or so and planting three hundred (yes, I said "hundred") dahlias. I've planted a few dahlias in my day only to discover just how much work they are. "Oh, he and his buddy would do all the work" he assured me.

"What about weeds?" I demanded. "And digging the dahlias up in the fall? And where are you going to store the tubers over the winter?" He had an answer for every one of my objections. And so, the following spring, I watched with trepidation as he and his buddy sacrificed valuable fishing time to plow and prepare the ground for their new flower bed.

By late summer, the dahlias were at their peak. Every relative, friend and acquaintance was invited to view my husband's dahlias. Proudly he led our visitors past my roses; down to the stunning new dahlia bed. Every conversation that summer began and ended with the word "dahlia". My enthusiasm was tepid. "This is a one-trick wonder," I told myself.

Eventually, I had to concede that early morning strolls through my husband's dahlias gave me the same sense of wonder and joy I experienced when wandering through my own garden creations.

It's hard to let others into our special places. We think no one cares as much as we do. We think we know best. We don't want to patch up another's mistakes or finish what they leave undone. But, being willing to share the spotlight just might brighten everyone's day.

Purpose

My aunt had a talent for placing the right plant in just the right spot. The long row of iris she planted beside her driveway served as my inspiration when we relocated to our new home in western Montana. I hoped to use iris, as she had done, to create a showy border somewhere on our newly acquired property.

The eastern boundary of my vegetable garden, in plain view of my office window, seemed to be the logical location. Once established, the border created a beautiful splash of color and provided a growing barrier between the yard and the hay fields beyond. In addition, rototilling between the iris, the lawn and my garden plot would waylay the unrelenting invasion of quack grass.

Over the years, in every way, the iris fulfilled the purpose I had in mind for them. Announcing, with dramatic, colorful blooms, the official arrival of summer, my iris border presented an image of glorious perfection.

Just as my purpose for the iris, so is God's purpose for us. Exercising our purpose gives our lives focus and meaning. Early on, we should identify God's will and live accordingly. Asking questions will help clarify our purpose. Why am I here? What are my strengths, weaknesses and talents? Am I on the right track? Can I get back on track?

Living our purpose requires vision, discipline and creativity. Often, we are misguided, investing a great deal of time and energy into activities we are ill-suited for. Periodically, it is good to do a personal inventory. Scripture, our friends and family members, as well as our own personal compass, can help us find the unique purpose He intends for each of us.

Now is a good time to give some thought to your purpose. Discover your God-given gifts and then use them to live your life with enthusiasm and determination.

*"My purpose is that they may be encouraged
in heart and united in love ..."*

COLOSSIANS 2:2

purpose ~ iris   35

"...the Spirit intercedes for the saints in accordance with God's will."

Intercede

Nothing in the plant world attracts my attention like big, bold, blue hydrangeas. My son and new daughter-in-law had a spectacular one next to the back door of their first home in Seattle. My plan to take a piece of it home to Montana was thwarted when they suddenly moved to Singapore.

I tried growing my own but, in spite of promises that the plant would bloom blue, it never happened. I had good luck with the snowball and lace cap hydrangeas, both elegant but definitely not blue. People in the "know" told me I had the wrong type of soil and that blue blossoms were an unrealistic expectation. Others suggested I could intercede in the process by adding aluminum sulfate to the soil surrounding the hydrangea, thus providing the minerals needed to produce blue blooms.

"But will it work?" I asked the garden center clerk. He assured me that it would. We concluded the sale with a jumbo box of the mysterious powder and another thriving, potted hydrangea. The plant is not big or bold yet but the consistent application of aluminum sulfate is producing the desired blue blossoms. Time should do the rest.

Intercession is often necessary in the human family as well. Sometimes it's called "sticking your nose into other people's business". Oftentimes it's unwelcome. Occasionally, it makes all the difference. Do you have something to offer those trying to work out life's difficulties? Do you care enough to get involved? Be fearless. Intercede, plead and pray on behalf of those who are struggling. Your loving support may be just what's needed. That, and a little time.

"The Lord reigns, let the earth be glad; let the distant shores rejoice."

PSALMS 97:1

Rejoice

There is always cause for rejoicing when you get more than you bargained for, which is exactly what happened when I bought a shriveled up Oriental Lily at my local grocery store. The lilies had been on display for some weeks, but while I marveled at their beauty, I recoiled at their price tag.

Finally, as summer came to a close, the store marked the few remaining plants down to half price and left them to fend for themselves. By the time I had opened my check book, gotten the plant home and in the ground, it seemed like a loosing proposition, even at half the price.

But, my, oh, my! What a surprise the following summer when the lily came bursting forth in all its splendor and glory. I hadn't noticed its early efforts to climb up above the surrounding plants, but suddenly there it was: tall, proud and spectacular.

With very little effort on our part we are treated to a continual stream of glorious surprises. From the majesty of the natural world, the miraculous benefits of man's technology, to the warmth of the human heart, we profit mightily from God's handiwork. Rejoice, and again I say, rejoice!

Plan

You can make a lot of mistakes when you are more interested in "doing" than "planning". I bought this beautiful rocket plant for the flower bed out along the driveway, to the west of the house. I could not have picked a worse spot. Exposed to the afternoon sun and the dry soil, the poor thing nearly died.

Finally, after a couple of years of wondering why this once vigorous plant was looking so bedraggled and frumpy, I went to my garden book and read that the plant needed damp, boggy soil. Better late than never, I got busy and moved it to my flower bed next to the back yard water spigot.

As the summer progressed, the rocket plant's foliage turned a glossy, vibrant green. The stems spiked to about five feet tall and were crowned with hundreds of tiny yellow blossoms. Since then, the plant has been the focal point of that flower bed, enhancing and accenting all the other flowers surrounding it.

Creation requires planning. A life change demands forethought. As each day dawns, it calls for some preparation and scheduling. Good intentions will not carry the day. The more noble the purpose, the more carefully we should plan.

A goal without a plan is only a dream. To accomplish something worthwhile, we must begin with noble motives, plan carefully and then act with certitude and confidence. Well laid strategies, implemented religiously, will carry us to our goal, be it a new flower bed or a pilot's license!

"But the noble man makes noble plans and by noble deeds he stands."

Truth

To be honest, I don't know what happened in this flower bed. All I can say for sure is that I planted about two dozen pastel tulip bulbs which, gradually, over three or four years, were replaced by huge, dramatic, purple alliums.

What happened to the tulip bulbs? Where did the alliums come from? I wish I knew. Time has fogged my memory. Maybe I planted alliums along with the tulips and just forgot. Would digging up the flower bed answer these questions? Probably not. The truth is, once I had tulips; now I have alliums. Why or how this happened will remain a mystery.

I had three options: digging up the flower bed and starting over, forgetting the tulips while enjoying the alliums or, planting more tulips in and around the alliums. My choice could not rely on the unanswered questions of yesterday, but on the results I desire in the future.

In nearly every situation, "truth" is hard to nail down. Memories prove unreliable. Events or actions can be misinterpreted. Everyone's perspective is different. We can keep digging, interrogating, investigating and hypothesizing but, without verifiable facts, the events of yesterday are just the makings of a good story.

Half truths, rumors, gossip or fantasy should have no influence on today's decisions. What do you hope to accomplish? Are you trying to mend a relationship, forge a bond or rebuild trust?

The success of such endeavors depends on establishing elementary facts and acknowledging reality. Acting on what we can discern as "the truth" will eventually lead to a more trustworthy outcome. Discernment, the art of looking beyond the obvious, is always more productive than speculation. Only the foolish fool themselves and others. Proverbs tells us that the folly of fools is deception but "wisdom resides in the heart of the discerning."

"They must keep hold of the deep truths of the faith with a clear conscience."

I Timothy 3:9

"He will take great delight in you; He will quiet you with His love . . ."

Zephaniah 3:17

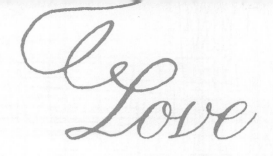

Nothing says it better. World wide the rose is a symbol of desire, passion and adoration. It is a gift for the beautiful and a reward for the accomplished. The rose is gathered into dozens and placed in the arms of beauty queens, formed into a horseshoe shape and draped around the neck of winning race horses or strewn by tiny flower girls into the pathway of brides.

Growing in the garden the rose whispers love to the sojourner. With its gentle, quiet beauty, it reminds us of the sweetness and splendor of true love, the kind of love that lasts beyond fascination or obsession. Rose petals, as soft as a lover's touch, shimmering in the morning light, cause us to pause and consider the sort of love that created such perfection.

A day that begins with the delightful sight and aroma of a rose in full bloom speaks to me of God's love for all of His creation. A rose bud, wrapped as delicately as a baby in the womb, is God's promise for a blessed tomorrow.

My advice to a busy world: throw out the alarm clock, rise a few minutes early and immerse yourself in something lovely. Snuggle with your children, meditate on scripture, take a quiet walk, or dance in the kitchen. Express your love to your creator and to his creation. Make this the beginning of a perfect day.

Transformed

When we first moved into our old farm house it was heated primarily with an old Franklin stove. Each fall we chopped and stacked enough firewood to get us through the winter. By spring we had piles of wood chips and, sometimes, unused wood. Grass would not grow up through the mess, but weeds would. Cleaning it up, I told myself, was pointless; since the process would begin all over again the following fall.

Eventually we replaced the wood stove with gas heat. Now, I no longer had any excuse for not tackling the eastern boundary of our yard.

We started by stacking the unused wood behind the shop. What could not be hauled away, I raked to the edge of the hay field and burned. Next, we planted grass. Since hardly anyone ventured around to the east side of the house, I decided not to invest a lot of money and time in landscaping the project. I did have a pile of daylilies someone had given me, which I casually stuck in along the foundation of the house.

It took a couple of years but what a transformation. I now invite guests to circle the whole house and, with pride, show off my lovely daylilies as they flaunt their summer blossoms eastward, toward the mountains.

Whether it's loosing a dress size, rebuilding a relationship, or painting a bedroom, change takes work. There is no magic, only sweat, married to the clock or calendar. Start the transformation now. As the old saying goes, "begin and you are half done".

*"...be transformed
by the renewing of
your mind."*

Shout

It's commonly called a trumpet plant. My first one was given to me by my sister-in-law. "Put it where it gets lots of sun," she advised. Since it would bloom white, the south side of the house, right at the end of my moonlight flower bed, seemed like the perfect spot.

Early on, I learned that the trumpet plant has the personality of an extrovert and a show-off! Given lots of water, heat and sunshine, its growth is fast and dramatic. Everyone who came and went during the hot summer months of August and September stopped to admire the newest addition to my front flower bed. With blossoms the size of dinner plates it seemed that, if called on, the trumpet shaped blooms could bring down the walls of Jericho.

Sometimes, but not often, everything falls into place. It might be a modest accomplishment. Maybe you caught the biggest fish or finally got that bashful two year old nephew to sit on your lap. Maybe you managed to meet your pastor's challenge to read the whole Bible in a year. Or possibly an epic battle has been won, an addiction conquered, a prize awarded! Celebrate, my friend! God intends for us to enjoy the abundant life He promised us.

A modest and humble demeanor is admirable but there is no sin in tooting your own horn occasionally! Take a bow. Brag just a little! Sometimes we are faster, smarter, bigger, and better than we ever imagined ourselves to be. Shout, rejoice, and be glad for each and every victory!

"Shout aloud, O Israel! Be glad and rejoice with all your heart!"

ZEPHANIAH 3:14

shout ~ trumpet

"But one thing I do: forgetting what is behind and straining toward what is ahead I press on..."

PHILIPPIANS 3:13

forget ~ tulip

Forget

My nieces and nephew ordered lots of yellow tulips for their mother's funeral. It was her favorite flower. And so, in the dead of winter, yellow tulips were everywhere. What a beautiful reminder, that even in death, we can celebrate life.

As I watch the tulips in my own garden sprout, bloom and then fade, I'm reminded that spring is coming to a close. I'm not ready for summer. The flowers, the trees, the green grass and even the air I breathe, are just too glorious to leave behind. But in spite of my objections, the tulips crumble and die; the days get longer and warmer.

The loss of my cheerful tulips is soon forgotten as the peonies, poppies, delphiniums and lupine begin to bloom. It's then the real work begins. Weeds burst forth, sprinklers and hoses must be set and moved regularly and the lawn demands mowing. Fertilizing, mulching and dead heading are regular ongoing tasks. Summer sweeps you up in its arms and drags you into autumn. By that time you are tired; ready to put the garden to bed. The wonder and thrill of spring and the demanding work load of summer are replaced with the fatalism of fall. It's with a sense of relief that you cover the last rose, rake the leaves and wait for that first snowflake.

Our life span is very much like the seasons. Maybe by this time, you realize that it's best to keep pressing forward. Whatever the season of life, be it young, middle age or old, it is good to forget the mistakes and missed opportunities of yesterday. We still have work to do and blessings to enjoy. There will be time enough in the winter of life for the recliner, a warm fire and a good book.

Hope

Once upon a time, Memorial Day was referred to as "Decoration Day". In that long ago era, there were no artificial flowers. Bouquets could not be ordered by phone and delivered "FTD". Even so, there were babies to be remembered, fallen soldiers to be memorialized and deceased parents to be honored.

My Grandmother, Aunt and Mother began preparations the night before Decoration Day. In the cool of the evening they moved through their individual yards, gathering whatever flowers were available that last weekend in May. Mostly they were lilacs. Buckets of the sweet smelling blooms, some purple, some white, filled the trunk as we drove up the hill to the graveyard above town.

While weeds were pulled, stiff prairie grass clipped and water sloshed into foil wrapped coffee cans, Grandma systematically divided the lilacs, tulips and iris so that each grave she felt responsible for, either by blood, marriage or just plain good will, was decently decorated.

As her grandchildren helped place coffee can bouquets at each head stone she related, at their urging, stories about the departed one and their place in our family history.

"Did they go to heaven?" was the most often asked question. "I hope so," was her most likely response.

Hope is faith in the future. What speaks more plainly of hope than the lilac? Regardless of the length or the severity of the winter, does anyone doubt that the lilacs will bloom each and every spring?

Yes, it seems to us mortals that the graveyard is the end. But we can have hope in God's promise of salvation and eternal life. Our Father has ordered the universe, the seasons and growing things so that hope is always on the horizon. What appears to be the end of our life path is simply a curve in the road. Be of good cheer! Good things are just around the bend.

"... the Lord delights in those who fear Him, who put their hope in His unfailing love."

PSALMS 147:11

hope ~ lilac

About the Author

Kareen Bratt, a Montana native, writes eloquently of her experiences growing and living in such a wild and wonderful place as her home state. Growing up on a wheat farm in the high plains and then moving with her family to the rugged and beautiful Flathead Valley, Kareen has been able to draw inspriation from the stunning beauty and sometimes tough way of life Montana offers its citizens. She shares that inspiration in the form of life lessons the rest of us would otherwise miss.

Also by Kareen Bratt:
My Home's in Montana: Memoir of a Ranch Family

Drama, danger, delight and disappointment draws the reader into an era and a way of life nearly unknowable except to the hardy few who still stake their claim to the prairies of Montana.

Growing up on a wheat ranch, without the distractions of TV or computers, Kareen developed a knack for distilling adult conversations and actions. In this fast moving memoir, Kareen transports the reader into the calculating minds of young children intent on outwitting (at least in the short run) parents, teachers, grandparents and even a few neighbor ladies. These were children who lived most of their waking hours outdoors, devising their own entertainment and rules of engagement.

Told with the authenticity of one who remembers with great affection, the wind, sky and land of her ranch home, the reader can almost feel the chill of an early morning run to the outhouse or the heat of a harvest kitchen.

Made in the USA
Charleston, SC
03 June 2015